IMAGES
of England

HARWICH AND DOVERCOURT

Engraved for RAYMOND's *History of England.*

Dodd delin. Collyer sculp.

Her Majesty QUEEN CHARLOTTE *landing at* HARWICH, *on her way to St James's Palace Sep.r 7. 1761.*

Queen Charlotte arriving at Harwich, 7 September 1761. Due to unfavourable weather, the voyage from Holland had taken ten days. The then princess was accompanied by a fleet of five royal yachts (one seen in the background) and was welcomed at Harwich by the mayor and aldermen. She was on her way to St James Palace to be received by King George III as his young bride.

IMAGES
of England

HARWICH AND DOVERCOURT

Compiled by
John Mowle

TEMPUS

First published 2001
Copyright © John Mowle, 2001

Tempus Publishing Limited
The Mill, Brimscombe Port,
Stroud, Gloucestershire, GL5 2QG

ISBN 0 7524 2208 1

Typesetting and origination by
Tempus Publishing Limited
Printed in Great Britain by
Midway Colour Print, Wiltshire

Harwich Quay, c. 1900. Jack Good's fishing bawley, alongside, with a salvaged yacht. In the background are the newly erected Great Eastern refreshment rooms, Tendring Hundred waterworks building and two lads swimming in the pound – much as they do today.

Contents

An aerial view of Harwich and Dovercourt in the 1960s.

Acknowledgements

The author thanks the following for their help: Dave Tricker, Cheryl Thompson, Henry Manning, Arthur and Peggy Chambers, Elizabeth Walters, Joan Gates, Rosemary Potts, Frank Humphries, Mrs Gostling, Lil Sneddon, Bruce and Jane Pennick and Mrs Howlett.

Introduction

Harwich stands on a narrow peninsula in north-east Essex, at the mouth of the Rivers Stour and Orwell where they lead into the North Sea. It is a town of ancient and modern; its streets follow the grid system laid down in Medieval days, the three main streets lie north to south, the narrow streets joined by alleyways designed, it is said, to provide shelter from the easterly winds. These alleys and small yards nearly all take their names from the ancient gates of the town or from past owners and are reminiscent of past days. History tells that the town of Orwell was destroyed by the encroachment of the sea and upon the ruins of this Harwich grew. During the Middle Ages, Harwich was a place of great importance as it was the only harbour of refuge between the Thames and Humber and thought to be the best on the East Coast. In the reign of Edward II, it was made a Corporate Borough and the charter given was confirmed by succeeding monarchs. James I granted a more ample charter 'for the Borough of Harwich and Dovercourt'. The Scottish king also restored to the borough the power of returning two members to Parliament, a privilege which had been discontinued since the days of Edward III.

Daniel Defoe, on one of his visits to Harwich, noted that; ' The inhabitants are far from being famed for good usage to strangers but, on the contrary, are blamed for being extravagant in their reckonings in the public houses'.

The 1950s proved to be a critical period for Harwich, the housing stock had been allowed to fall into disrepair and quite a number of dwellings were classed as unfit for habitation. The council made a decision to demolish vast numbers of inferior houses to provide space for commercial use and new housing. With the benefit of hindsight many now would question this decision. Unfortunately, in the 1960s-70s the council continued to demolish some unique buildings during which time the town lost the Quay Pavilion, the Royal Flats, Currents Lane and the Salvation Army home. Over a period of fifty years Harwich has lost almost half of its original buildings. However, the new development of Harwich Quay, the re-vamped Halfpenny Pier and the brand new Lifeboat station will, hopefully, help to bring prosperity back to the town. It's worth noting that in 1920 there were over one hundred and forty commercial premises in Harwich and thirty in Market Street alone.

My own interest in Harwich and Dovercourt stems from my youth, when I began to collect local history photographs and postcards. When asked to produce this book the task seemed daunting, but a few months (and 12,000 words of script) later, the deed is done and I find myself much wiser for the experience. Most of the pictures are from my own collection, with a few borrowed from friends, and I have found the research into subject matter both fascinating and enormously enjoyable. A great deal of information has been gleaned from local people who either remember facts and events themselves, or have had information passed down to them. I would like to thank these people, together with family and friends, for their input and interest, with very special thanks to Peter Goodwin for his support and encouragement, and for sacrificing his Wednesday evenings and Saturday mornings to assist in the research of this book.

John Mowle
March 2001

41 HOUSES SPLIT THIS TOWN!

MAJOR WOOD-POTTLE
"We intend to keep our town."

★

ERIC WAINWRIGHT

tells the story of a battle which the local newspaper headlined "HARWICH RISES IN ANGER"

★

Harwich, Essex, Friday.

"HELLO everyone, hello, everyone, Harwich Town is falling down."

The loudspeaker van, hired at £3 for the afternoon, moves down Market-street where every second building is derelict and flies swarm among the drowsy ruins.

"Mass meeting of protest tonight," blares the speaker. On the corner four grim housewives shout, "We'll be there."

The people of Harwich Town (pop. 4,191, one cinema twenty-two pubs) are seething with anger.

In Church-street eighty-five-year-old Bill Bryant shakes his stick at a boarded-up shop front.

"Nothing been done to that place since it burnt out in 1913."

✦ ✦ ✦

AND from the doorway of Ye Golden Galleon teashop Major Robert Wood-Pottle, the owner, nods agreement.

"For thirty years this town has been neglected and now the council have passed a scheme which will mean tearing down forty-one occupied houses and turning a quarter of the town into a buoy-yard."

The plan to move the Trinity House buoy department from Blackwall to Harwich was put up in 1944. Little was said of negotiations at the time because, as Councillor Bernard said, "Wives might write to husbands who would seek compassionate leave to come home because they were to be turned out of their house, and yet the thing might never happen."

But Harwich men say their town was sold behind their backs.

✦ ✦ ✦

FIRST news that the plan had been approved appeared in the local Press in April headed "Harwich Rises in Anger."

But at first it was no stronger than a mild muttering among the gaffers along the quayside

DR. GROOM
"I'll back you."

"Christopher Jones, cap'n of the Mayflower was born in one of they houses." grumbled Frank Goodey "It's part of our history."

In April Ron Monks banged a glass on his own counter at "The Globe."

"Why don't we do something. Let's form an association to fight the council."

"I'll back you," nodded Doctor Groom, owner of several of the doomed properties.

And three days later the first meeting of the Harwich Protection Association was held at "The Three Cups," where Nelson planned the battle of Copenhagen.

Things boiled up when a retired London policeman, Alec Reece, received a curt letter from a local estate agent on behalf of Trinity House suggesting an amicable agreement for the sale of his house, otherwise a compulsory order would be made.

"I didn't sleep for three nights.' says Mrs Reece "It's a lovely old sixteenth century house. We put all our savings into it when we came three years ago. And what's to become of my old parents who are living with us?"

✦ ✦ ✦

THE Protection Society headed by retired cavalryman Major Wood-Pottle. went into action The Society for the protection of Ancient Buildings promised full support, but a suggestion that the Duke of Gloucester be invited to see the state of the town was turned down by Mayor Horn.

The council argue that the proposed buoy-yard will bring trade to the town. The people say that a quarter of their town is too big a price to pay and suggest that Trinity House use the vacant land at Bathside, a mile away.

And on Wednesday they declared war on the Town Hall. Posters advertised a mass meeting at the Quay Pavilion, and all afternoon the loudspeaker van trailed through the streets An hour before the meeting the 500 seats were filled, and when it began 700 people crowded the hall, and 200 stood outside in the late evening sun

✦ ✦ ✦

THEY were earnest and anxious. They were unanimous in rejecting the Trinity House scheme and unanimous in passing a vote of no confidence in the council.

"And now we sha' tackle the Home Office,' says Major Wood-Pottle "We like our town and we intend to keep it."

RON MONKS
"Fight the council."

One
Maritime Harwich

Jack Good aboard the salvaged yacht. The broken mast can be clearly seen as well as temporary repairs to the port side bow. Canvas and tar were used to cover the damage. In the background is Halfpenny Pier.

Royal Navy steam tenders arrive at Halfpenny Pier in 1906. The view upstream features a visiting warship and across the pound is the Continental Pier, built in 1886. A schooner alongside and an early lightship can be seen on the opposite side of the pier.

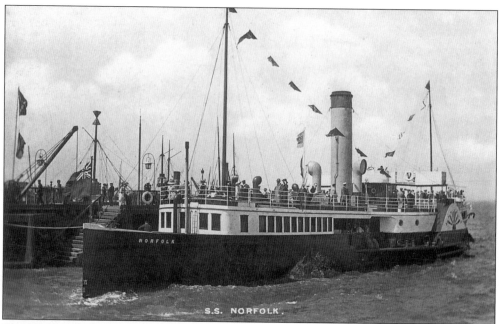

The SS *Norfolk* departs from the pier with another group of day-trippers to Ipswich, *c.* 1910. Several paddle steamers worked this route, each carrying 150 passengers. These excursions were very popular and on Bank Holidays the steamers worked to full capacity all day. Felixstowe was another destination.

The *Yvonne* pleasure launch arriving back at Harwich with a group of day-trippers in the 1950s. Ralph Potts, the owner, is at the helm. The most popular trip was to the Reserve Fleet moored up river at Parkeston Quay.

MV *Brightlingsea* disembarking passengers at Halfpenny Pier from Felixstowe in 1936. The *Brightlingsea* was built in 1925 by the Rowhedge Shipbuilding Co. and was operated by LNER and British Rail, working the Felixstowe-Harwich route. Mr Goodhew took over the service when BR ceased operating in 1962; later Alan Pridmore took over the vessel and ran the service together with river cruises until 1997 when it ceased to be profitable. The boat was, until recently, laid up and in a sad state of repair at Walton Backwaters.

The 'Twins' MV *Epping* and MV *Hainault*; identical boats built at Portsmouth in 1914, moored at Halfpenny Pier in the 1950s. Each was 50ft long and weighed 11.8 tons and both were used on the Shotley-Felixstowe-Harwich passenger service until the early 1960s. Both boats survive, albeit in poor condition.

A Royal Navy trot boat leaves the pier around 1914 loaded with army personnel who were possibly returning to Landgaurd Fort, across the estuary at Felixstowe.

A view from Harwich Quay around 1910 with the steam lifeboat *City of Glasgow II* and a steam launch moored alongside. A paddle steamer arriving from Ipswich and several barges add to a busy harbour scene. The large ship moored in the river is the guardship HMS *Mersey*.

The tug *Revenged* in the early 1920s, trapped in Gas House Creek, Harwich, by a paddle minesweeper grounded across the entrance. The tug had come from London to tow the minesweeper clear of the entrance.

Empire Lucy, Birch Class tug on the slip at Harwich for repairs in the early 1950s. This was one of several tugs based at Harwich and used jointly by the Ministry of Transport and the Admiralty between 1946 and 1958. In 1962 she was released by the Admiralty and sold to maritime Augustea Spa and renamed *Ognina* in 1972. She was still in use in the late 1980s.

Empire Lucy having damage repaired at Harwich Navyard. The massive propeller had lost one of its blades.

The boiler room of *Empire Lucy*; the boiler is being stoked by Lenny 'the lick' Alexander.

Empire Race moored at Harwich in 1945. *Race* was built in 1941 and run by Rowbottom & Sons London, who also managed *Lucy*, *Teak* and *Cedar*. She was employed on naval duties at Harwich 1945-1958. She was a Birch Class tug, of which many were built.

Sailing barge *Edith May* in Harwich Harbour, *c.* 1950. Built in 1906 by J. & H. Cann of Harwich, she was named after Edith May Cann and was 64 tons, length 85ft and beam 20ft. With the Thames barge races, as well as trade in mind the Canns built the *Edith May* 'on spec', as they thought a barge should be built, not specifically to an owner's design, but to make the perfect racing shape. She is reckoned to be the strongest wooden barge ever built, as well as the fastest and prettiest, and is currently undergoing total restoration.

A view of the Pound seen from the Halfpenny Pier in the mid-1950s. The three Shrimpers are the *Molly Lass*, *Why Worry* and the *Girl Elsie*.

A view looking downstream to Harwich around 1950 showing the floating dock and the 'mothballed' gun. Alongside are several gunboats, (MGBs), which remained here until the 1960s.

HMS *Brinton*, a Coniston class minehunter and part of 104 Minesweeper Squadron, leaving for the Mediterranean, 25 August 1956. The SS *Vienna* is moored alongside at Parkeston Quay.

Harwich Quay, early 1960s. A massive catch of sprats is being loaded for the fish canneries. On the quayside is Fred Good in oilskins; his son Victor is on board the trawler. The dredger *Landguard* is berthed alongside the Pier.

The Quay in the early 1950s. Arthur Smith of Harwich Lighters unloads ballast dredged from the river, which was used to build the footings for many local houses during the 1950s. Some of the Harwich Shrimpers are moored in the pound.

A seaplane of Aquila Airways photographed in the mid-1950s. This was the last commercial seaplane flight out of Harwich. The airline used Short Solent or Sunderland flying boats and had routes to Madeira and Las Palmas and also a freight service from Southampton to Australia. The company ceased trading in 1958.

Gas House Creek in the 1930s with the fishing bawley, *Autodafe* in the creek and train ferry No. 3 at the rail terminal. This bawley won many races and was certainly one of the fastest craft of its type.

Hydroplane hangars at Shotley, 1912. Landing rights were obtained in Harwich Harbour where trials and surveys were carried out. Commander Samson felt that the Felixstowe side of the river would be more suitable as a site for a seaplane base, and on the 5 August 1913 the operation was moved across the river to become known as Seaplanes-Felixstowe, commanded by Sqdn Comm. Charles Risk.

One of the hydroplanes moored off Shotley, c. 1911. Several pilots flew out of Shotley, including E. Connor and Lieut C.R. Samson. In 1912 *Ganges' boys* assisted in Samson's historic flight during the Weymouth review when he took off from the deck of HMS *Hibernia* which was steaming at 10.5 knots.

The Navyard in the 1950s, seen here shortly before it became known as Navyard Wharf. Steeped in history, this yard is where Sir Anthony Deane built a number of famous warships in the mid 1600s. The Royal Navy had the use of the yard in both world wars. The ketch *Startled Fawn* is pictured on the slipway.

Zeebrugge Train Ferry. Harwich.

96805

Train ferry at Harwich terminal, 1925. HRH Prince George opened the terminal on 24 April 1924 and the service continued until 1983.

HMS *Badger* in Harwich harbour 1941. The *Badger* was renamed when the Navy decided to bring her to Harwich. She was brought round to Harwich in 1939 and used to accommodate naval personnel and stores and stayed for the duration of the war. She was formerly A/V *Danfolk* and A/V *Westward*.

The Sunk Lightship, No. 85, mid-1930s. Trinity House Lights department, Harwich, was responsible for the maintenance of all lightships and buoys in British coastal waters. This light vessel is of the '80s' class and was moored about twelve miles off Harwich. She had a skipper

and six crew members who each worked for one month, followed by two weeks ashore. *The Sunk*'s sister ship No. 87, now houses a restaurant at Levington Marina.

German U-boats at Harwich after their surrender on 20 November 1918. More than 150 of these, plus support craft, arrived at Harwich. Each submarine had a White Ensign hoisted above the German flag and amongst the subs were some of the latest types, over 300ft long.

HMS *Mersey*, a coastguard ship moored at Harwich in 1894. The *Mersey* was built at Chatham dockyard in 1885. Her speed was 17.3 knots and she was commanded by Capt. George W. Hill. She had three sister ships the *Thames*, *Forth* and *Severn*. The *Severn* also served at Harwich.

Two
Old Harwich

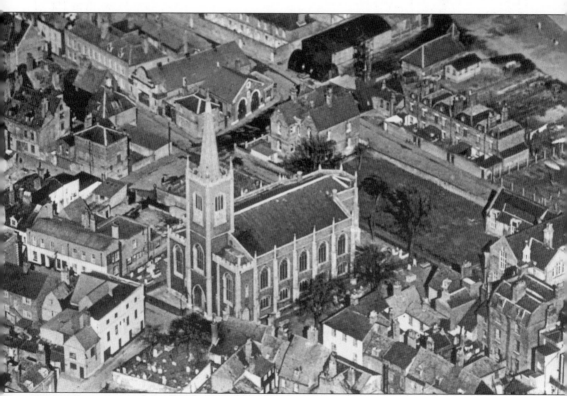

St Nicholas church, Harwich, early 1950s. Rebuilt in 1820, it was a main landmark and navigational aid. Famous visitors to the original church (which was founded in 1177 by Roger Bigod First Earl of Norfolk) were sailors Drake, Howard and Nelson, and local MP Samuel Pepys. Still in existence today are the records of the two marriages of Christopher Jones, captain of the *Mayflower*.

Great Eastern and Pier hotels viewed from the Halfpenny Pier, *c.* 1912. At the centre of the Great Eastern, the Royal Harwich Yacht Club's flag can be seen, which, when in line with the chequered flag on the pier, determined the starting line for the yacht races. Here a race is in progress; several spectators line the quayside.

A crowd on Harwich Quay awaiting the arrival of Ipswich and Felixstowe pleasure boats, early 1900s.

Halfpenny Pier thronged with would-be passengers for the Ipswich steam ferries in the early 1900s. Training ship HMS *Ganges* can be seen moored in the river. Note the policeman at the turnstiles.

The Quay Pavilion, 1950s. This was previously the refreshment rooms belonging to the Great Eastern Hotel which were built to accommodate passengers waiting to board the ferries. The Quay Pavilion was demolished in the early 1970s to make way for Trinity House workshops and offices.

The harbour master's office in 1920. Mr J.W. Holmes (deputy harbour master 1901-1924), Mr Bradman and his dog wait outside the new premises of the Conservancy Board that adjoins Naval House in Kings Quay Street. The building was demolished in 1960 for development of the Navyard.

Groom's drinking fountain, c. 1910. This ornate structure was erected in 1904 and funded by Ald. Groom. Unfortunately an explosion in 1946, caused by a build up of gas, completely destroyed the fountain, which was never replaced.

A view looking towards West Street in the 1930s. Mr Keeble owned the 'Cash Boot' repair shop. Adjoining this was the Salvation Army Citadel and opposite on the right are the Royal Ordnance buildings, a small part of which was used by the Cann family as a shrimp processing factory.

The same view as above in the mid-1950s. By this time the shop and Ordnance buildings had disappeared; this site was later occupied by Bernard's offices.

The rear yard of the Elephant & Castle public house, 1910. A popular attraction was the aviary where an assortment of birds was housed. A parrot can be seen in the cage to the right. Posing for the camera we see the proprietor Mr George Baker on the left.

The Elephant & Castle Public House, c. 1950, situated in West Street. This pub was purpose built by Tollemache & Co around 1905, and replaced the original building which traded as a pub and alehouse in the mid-nineteenth century. Now called The Haywain, it retains its original external appearance.

An Edwardian scene, c. 1910. Clematis Courtyard at the Three Cups Hotel was overlooked from above by 'Nelson's Room'. On the anniversary of the planting of this fine clematis (1851) the hotel held carnivals with music and dancing and the tree was decorated with Chinese lanterns and flags.

Nelson's Room, Three Cups Hotel, c. 1910. Many famous people have enjoyed hospitality at this ancient establishment. Contrary to local belief there are no documents to prove that either Queen Elizabeth I or Lord Nelson actually stayed here.

Alexander the Great clothing store in around 1929, provider of clothing and oilskins to the local fishermen and seafarers. The store was situated at No. 50 Church Street. Pictured is the manager Mr Mayhew with his wife and child. In the 1960s the shop became Anglia Marine Agencies Ltd owned by Mr Donald Murrison.

Church Street Harwich in its heyday, c. 1910. A wealth of shops is evident among which are the Home & Colonial stores, Woodward's chemist, Stead & Simpson, Bodgener's clothing, Jackson the printers and Mead's bakers and confectioners.

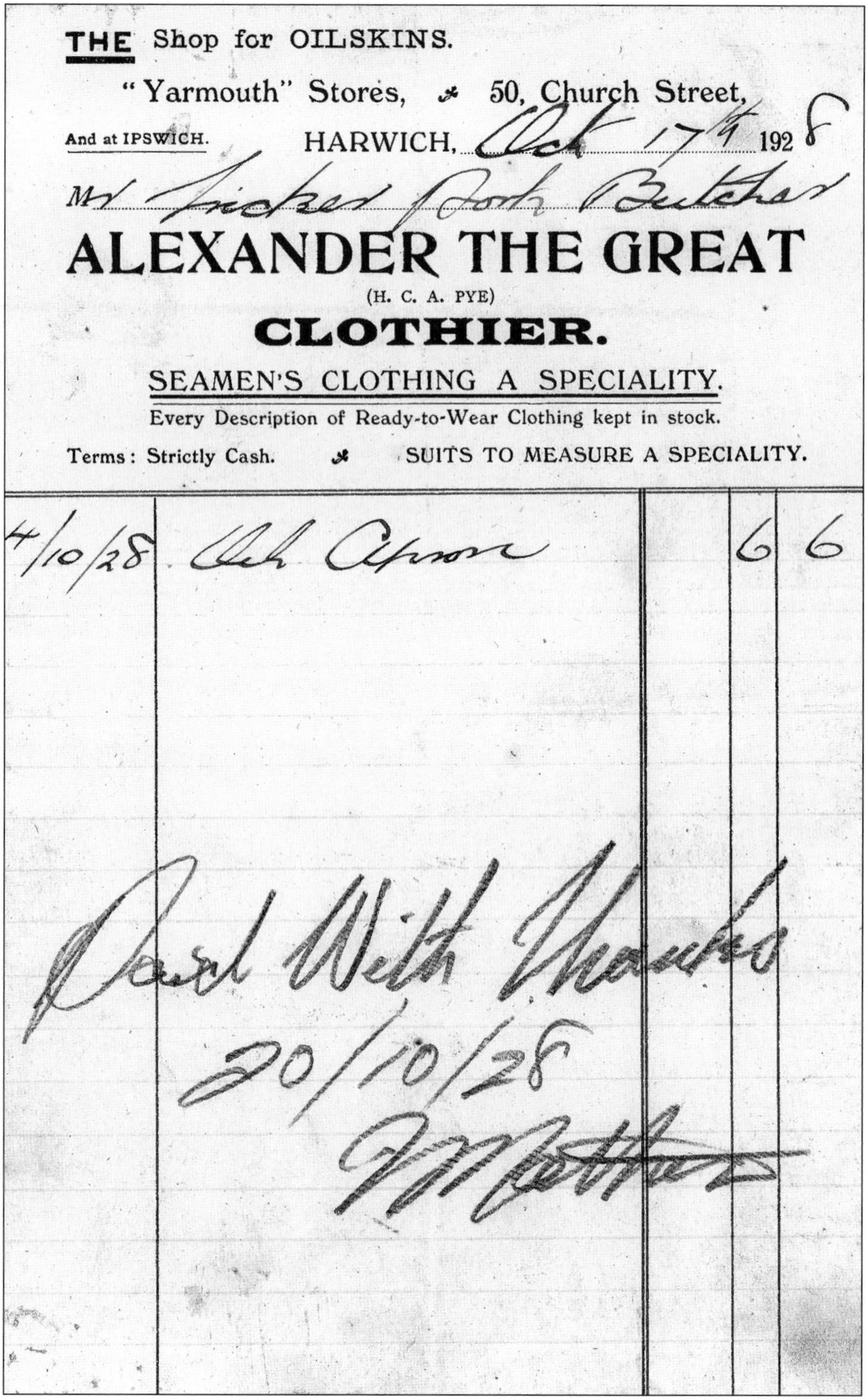

THE Shop for OILSKINS.

"Yarmouth" Stores, 50, Church Street,

And at IPSWICH. HARWICH, Oct 17th 1928

Mr Fisher Pork Butcher

ALEXANDER THE GREAT

(H. C. A. PYE)

CLOTHIER.

SEAMEN'S CLOTHING A SPECIALITY.

Every Description of Ready-to-Wear Clothing kept in stock.

Terms: Strictly Cash. SUITS TO MEASURE A SPECIALITY.

4/10/28	Oil Apron		6	6

Paid With Thanks
20/10/28

An Alexander the Great invoice of 1928.

The Market Place, 1929. Many shops were situated in this area including Tom Jones antiques, Vince & Sons bootmakers, Calver auctioneers, Jennings fishmongers and Whatling general stores. The area was demolished in 1938.

John Self ironmongers shop, No. 12 Kings Quay Street around 1910, showing Mr Self outside with his son. He may also have owned the china shop opposite at No. 12 St Austin's Lane. Number 12 Kings Quay Street is now the Sign of the Bear restaurant.

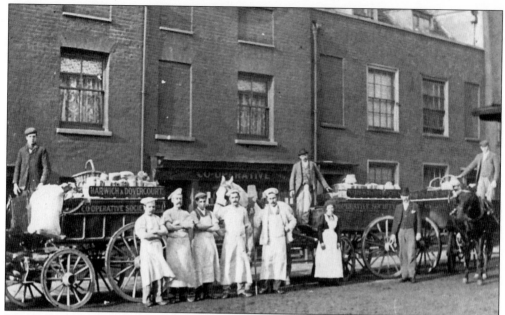

The Co-op Bakery, West Street, *c.* 1915. Bakery workers relax to have their picture taken. Mr Carter owned these premises, baking bread for the Co-op. Later, the Co-op moved to a new building in Grafton Road. In 1923 the shop became a greengrocers, owned by Mr Andreotti. The property remained empty after his death until Stan Humphries opened it up again as a bakery. In 1962 Mr Humphries' son Frank took over the business and runs it to this day with his son Mark. 'Humphries' is the only independent baker trading in Harwich today. In the early 1800s the premises were an alehouse called the Six Bells.

David Wills' bakery, Kings Head Street, 1935. Mr Wills puts a fresh tray of ketchels into the oven in preparation for the mayor-making ceremony. The bakery was directly behind his shop and tearooms in Church Street. He also owned the Cake Shop at Upper Dovercourt, which was managed by his sister. David Wills was awarded several gold medals for the quality of his baking.

Tricker's shop during the 1920s. Mr W.H. Tricker was an entrepreneur who, at one time, owned or had an interest in twenty-eight businesses. This shop was a pork butchers selling brawn, ham, bacon, pies and sausages, all of which were made and cooked on the premises. Two of his staff are pictured here. The shop to the left was a hairdresser and perfumery under the name of Sid Cobb. On the right is the Royal Navy Outfitters. At the rear of Tricker's shop could be found a huge cold room, smokehouse and ice cream preparation area. The business was established in 1879.

A Tricker's pork pie wrapper.

The Old Curiosity Shop, Outpart Eastward, c. 1915. This shop adjoined the Coastguard station accommodation and sold china, bric-a-brac etc. A mural depicting nautical themes of Harwich has now been painted on the wall, which can be seen to the right of the picture.

An advertising card for the Old Curiosity Shop. Mr T. West-Carnie, who wrote many local history books and guides, owned this shop.

Johnny Barker making humbugs in the 1950s. His sweet shop was a child's paradise in those days. Mr Barker used to travel with Thurstons fair before opening his shop and was at one time, manager of the Electric Palace cinema.

Owen Coates' music shop, Church Street in around 1920. Coates, who lived in Lee Road, was a photographer producing local postcards. Sheet music, early gramophones and pianos can be seen in the shop windows. To attract customers a pianist would be employed to play in the shop. The shop was demolished after the Second World War and replaced with flats.

Capt. Gerald Curteis laying the foundation stone to the new Trinity House offices and operations room, 14 June 1951. The buildings are situated between Kings Head Street and Church Street at the Quay end and replaced warehouses previously on the site.

Harwich Lifeboat house seen here in around 1957, was built in 1876 to house the Springwell Lifeboat. The turret, removed in 1957-1958 was not, as is generally believed, either ornamental or a watchtower, but was in fact a sail-drying loft. The oar and sail lifeboat, when pulled inside, would have its mast hoisted so that the sail could dry out. The building is now a lifeboat museum.

George Driffill with his horse and cart, *c.* 1915. Mr Driffill used to travel miles selling goods from his cart loaded with all the consumables that the ordinary household would ever need. This photograph was taken in West Street, Harwich.

George Driffill with his family in around 1915, seen outside the fire station at the junction with Wellington Road. It may be George's day off, but as the same horse appears in the above picture, there is apparently no rest for him!

Tom Brewster's bakers shop, c. 1920. Mr Brewster was known locally as 'Uncle Tom'. Seen outside the shop are the baking staff who were, from left to right: Ethel Humpries, the baker's boy, and Stan Humpries. During the depression in the 1920s, 'Uncle Tom' was always ready with a huge supply of free hot soup and unsold bread to be given away to the needy.

A print of Harwich as viewed from the Cliffs in 1830. People are gathering copperas on the beach. St Nicholas church is in the middle of the view.

Cox's Pond, viewed from main road, *c.* 1920. This was a horse pond until approximately 1903 when the land was purchased in order to landscape it into an ornamental duck pond. Note the unhindered view to the Redoubt Fort, before Harbour Crescent was built.

Staff of International Tea Company's shop, Market Street, *c.* 1928. This was later used by Cann's ships chandlers until closure in the 1980s. The shop premises have since been converted into one large house.

The Singer sewing machine shop, Church Street, *c.* 1920. Apprentice sewing machine mechanic Charles Gooch is seen astride his Invicta motor cycle.

The winter of 1954 was particularly severe, as this picture shows. Gas House Creek had frozen over, a sight rarely seen.

The Wheatsheaf public house, *c.* 1950. This was claimed to be the only Co-op pub in the country and incorporated the Co-op confectionery shop. The pub was previously known as the Co-op Tavern, and was sold to a private buyer in the 1960s. It is now known as the Stingray.

H.W. Gould's bakers cart, *c.* 1912. Mr Gould's shop was at No. 6 Kings Quay Street, adjacent to the Globe Inn. He was renowned for his 'Ships' biscuits.

A. Farrow, pork butcher, No. 44 Church Street, *c.* 1920. Farrow was known as the 'Sausage King' as the sign above indicates. His shop was one of four pork butchers in the town. The staff pictured outside includes the delivery boy with his trade bike. Part of this shop is now Good's fish shop run by Victor Good and his wife Barbara.

Royal Harwich Yacht Club, clubhouse and jetty, *c.* 1850. The Duke of York was elected Commodore in 1895 and HM George V was patron from 1910. Edward VII was a frequent visitor at the RHYC regattas with his racing yacht *Britannia*. An offer of a new permanent site at Cat House Hard, Wolverstone, was made to the club and accepted. The club moved to its new address in 1947-1948.

The White Hart Inn in February 1961, situated at No. 3 George Street at the junction with White Hart Lane. It overlooked the railway crossing, on the track that carried rail traffic to the trainferries. The White Hart closed as a pub in 1954 when the local Labour Party took it over, as its headquarters. Since demolished, the site is now residential.

The interior of the White Hart, c. 1920. This property boasted a most lavish interior, adorned with elegant grapevines and a very impressive balcony.

The Harwich Crane, *c.* 1930. This wheel crane was built in 1667 at the Navyard at a time when a number of warships were being constructed at Harwich. The crane worked on a tread wheel principle, operated by men walking in the interior of the wheel, as in the more familiar donkey wheels. There are two wheels in the crane, each wheel is 16ft in diameter and 3ft 10ins wide. The axle is of pitch pine and is roughly 14ins diameter - the jib projects 17ft 10ins. This photograph was taken shortly before the crane's re-siting to Harwich green.

The Wheel Crane re-erected on Harwich green in 1930. The crane was dismantled and reassembled here on a prepared site and rotten timbers were replaced. The reconstruction was supervised by Mr French the borough surveyor with the help of Mr D.W. Clark and with the craft and expertise of Mr F. Ainger, an old shipwright at the yard.

The construction of the Navyard Wharf, 1962. Previously a slipway as part of the shipbuilding yard, it had been in existence since 1657. Many ships were built here during the seventeenth and eighteenth centuries. Most of the yard was demolished in 1930 but it still continued to be used for marine associated work until 1960. The Navyard Wharf is still in existence and trading today.

To complete the Harwich section here is a comic postcard depicting Church Street in the 1920s.

Three
Dovercourt

Dovercourt High Street at the turn of the twentieth century, illustrating the early stages of its development into a shopping centre. Shops are just beginning to appear.

A Victorian view of High Street, *c.* 1897. Very few shops have yet appeared and houses still occupy the future Co-op site at Kingsway crossroads. A number of houses in Cliff Road are visible in the distance. In the foreground, on the left, is Birds bootmakers, and opposite is a confectioners, possibly Roch's. Wells the stationers can also clearly be seen.

A view from the west looking down High Street in around 1905. Davis the bakers is on the left-hand corner opposite the entrance to Mill Lane. Almost all of the properties on the right hand side from Mill Lane onwards, have since been demolished and replaced with modern shops and flats built in the 1960s and '70s.

The High Street approach to the Kingsway junction, *c.* 1925. The shop with the horse and cart outside belonged to J.A. Saunders the ironmonger, where many household requirements could be bought. The property was pulled down in the 1950s and the site is now occupied by National Westminster Bank, a travel agent, reframing shop and an insurance brokers. On the opposite side of the road we see the Gas and Coke Company offices, Saunders photographers and Christopher Jensen, outfitters.

The main High Street shopping area viewed from the crossroads in around 1920. As is evident from this scene, the High Street had grown considerably since 1900. All of the houses have become shops, partly due to the old established Harwich shop owners looking to the future and either moving their premises to Dovercourt or owning shops in both towns. The scene contains some prominent examples of advertising, note the banners of Thompson's and the café opposite, also a Kodak film advertisement on the wall of Dowdy's chemist shop.

Kingsway looking towards Marine Parade, c. 1912. At the bottom left hand corner is Pattinson's, drapers and milliners. The tower of the Kingsway Hall Evangelical church (built by Bagshaw) is a prominent feature. The Co-operative store and concert hall, built in 1902, is seen in the foreground. Just visible, top centre, is the Queen Victoria statue and at the top right hand side is the Alexandra Hotel. Kingsway was previously known as Stour Street and only twenty-five years earlier, was all but a narrow lane.

Leonard Gladstone Rice, tailors, of No. 82 High Street, c. 1920. This shop was erected in 1901 and was previously the premises of David Lambert, tailor and outfitter. Hughes Electrical now occupies this site.

Derelict houses in High Street, c. 1932. These were demolished shortly after this image was taken to make way for a new Woolworth's store. The tall building to the left was the Wesleyan chapel, built 1874, later used as sale rooms for Fred Rose & Son, auctioneers.

Woolworth's store, High Street in 1953. This store, known as the '3d & 6d Store' was built in 1934, the frontage being increased by roughly one half in 1937. Flags and bunting adorn the shop in honour of Queen Elizabeth's Coronation. Over the years Woolworths has undergone several facelifts and continues to trade here today.

John Buckle, grocer and wine merchant, 1922. Buckle's shop was located at Orwell House at the lower end of Orwell Terrace, and also had branches in London and Bognor Regis. Previous occupiers included Thompson and Self's grocery shop.

John Self's shops, No. 93 High Street, c. 1905. Self already owned two shops in Harwich when he opened these two in Dovercourt in 1904. The one on the left supplied ironmongery items the other sold china and cutlery. Several huge advertising lamps can be seen hanging outside. The property was situated between the International Tea Company and Went's bootmakers. Boots Chemists now occupies this site.

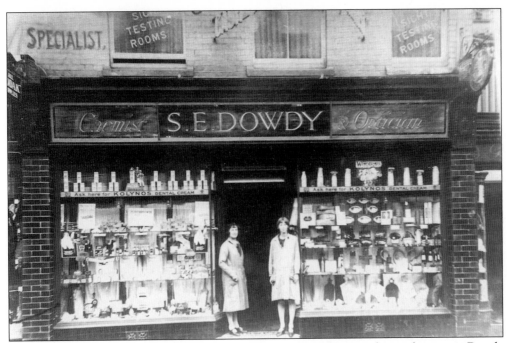

Sidney Dowdy's shop, No. 78 High Street, *c.* 1920, chemist, photographer and optician. Dowdy handled most of the developing and printing work in the town; even professional photographers used his services. Unwins wine merchants now occupy the shop.

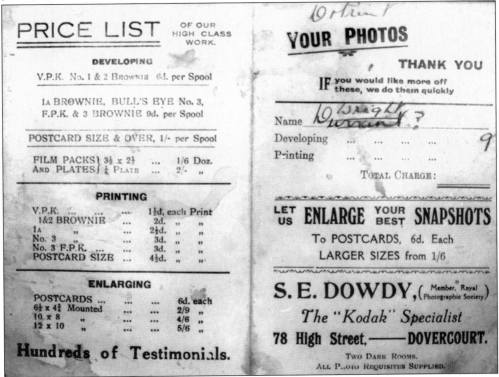

PRICE LIST OF OUR HIGH CLASS WORK.

DEVELOPING

V.P.K. No. 1 & 2 Brownie 6d. per Spool

1A BROWNIE, BULL'S EYE No. 3, F.P.K. & 3 BROWNIE 9d. per Spool

POSTCARD SIZE & OVER, 1/- per Spool

| FILM PACKS | 3½ x 2½ | ... | 1/6 Doz. |
| AND PLATES | ¼ Plate | ... | 2/- " |

PRINTING

V.P.K.	...	...	1½d. each Print
1 & 2 BROWNIE	...	2d.	" "
1A	"	...	2½d.	" "
No. 3	"	...	3d.	" "
No. 3 F.P.K.	...	3d.	" "
POSTCARD SIZE	...	4½d.	" "

ENLARGING

POSTCARDS	...	...	6d. each
6½ x 4½ Mounted	...	2/9 "
10 x 8	"	...	4/6 "
12 x 10	"	...	5/6 "

Hundreds of Testimonials.

YOUR PHOTOS

THANK YOU

IF you would like more off these, we do them quickly

Name ....

Developing ... ...

Printing ... ...

TOTAL CHARGE:

LET US ENLARGE YOUR BEST SNAPSHOTS

To POSTCARDS, 6d. Each

LARGER SIZES from 1/6

S. E. DOWDY, (Member, Royal Photographic Society)

The "Kodak" Specialist

78 High Street, ——— DOVERCOURT.

TWO DARK ROOMS.
ALL PHOTO REQUISITES SUPPLIED.

Dowdy's price list and photographic services.

Victoria Terrace as seen from High Street in 1911 was built by Robert Bagshaw in 1864 .The railway line passes close to the end of the street. Decorations indicate festivities on the occasion of King George V's coronation.

Lee Road facing the Cliff Hotel, *c.* 1920. Henry Lee purchased this land from Bagshaw's estate following the latter's bankruptcy. Lee began development in 1882 and after building a small number of houses in Lee Road, also became bankrupt. Chelmsford Land Company took over the project and completed the road, together with First, Second and Third Avenues.

Orwell Terrace and gardens in 1904, built by John Bagshaw around 1847. Bagshaw had been an East India merchant before becoming resident in Harwich around 1841. He then embarked on a very ambitious project – to build a new town at Dovercourt. He began by building a mansion named Cliff House and after a successful campaign, became MP for Harwich in 1847. After discovering that the grounds of Cliff House contained a chalybeate spring, he decided to build a spa and pump room, which were later to incorporate a library and reading room. He then went on to build Orwell Terrace, most of which still survives, mainly as flats.

Cliff Road in around 1913, looking towards Marine Parade. Development of Cliff Road began in around 1860 and consisted mainly of lodging houses and residences for professional people. The Congregational church was built in April 1908, along with the Sunday school. William Friese-Green, inventor of the first practical movie camera, occupied No. 5 Cliff Road from 1897-1904. Thomas Edison used Friese-Green's invention to produce his own camera, thus infringing his copyright. His invention was accepted and the film industry was launched; unfortunately Friese-Green received none of the credit, but went on to invent the inkless printing system, the forerunner of today's photocopier.

Marine Parade looking north in around 1899, most of which was built in the mid-1800s. A diversity of houses make up this Parade. At the far end is the Cliff Hotel. The tall mast seen behind, belonged to the Royal Navy Experimental Signalling Station and was made by the Navyard at Harwich and erected in the grounds of the Cliff Hotel. Marconi, the radio engineer, carried out experiments here whilst visiting Dovercourt on his yacht *Electra*, and later founded a radio school at Frinton-on-Sea.

The statue of Queen Victoria was built in 1903-1904 and unveiled 11 June 1904. This statue is of white marble on a grey granite pedestal and is situated along Marine Parade, facing Kingsway. There are some excellent examples here of typical modes of transport of the day!

Fronks Road, looking towards Marine Parade in the mid-1920s. Development of this part of Fronks Road began at the turn of the twentieth century. The donkeys make their weary way home after a long day giving pleasure rides to day-trippers along the Marine Parade. Their stables were in a field at the bottom of Blacksmiths Lane at Upper Dovercourt; quite a trek!

Dovercourt Bay railway station in 1908 was built to coincide with the opening of the railway line from London in 1854. The architecture remains very much unchanged today.

This view from around 1890 looks west along the lower promenade towards the lighthouses, just visible on the horizon. Top right are some of the first houses in Cliff Road, built in the mid-1860s. The slopes have yet to be landscaped and just one young family takes advantage of the path walks.

Marine Parade in the 1890s. This early photograph shows the initial stages of Bagshaw's development. Orwell Terrace and the Spa can be seen clearly in the background. The lower promenade, awaiting improvements, appears bleak and almost deserted. Two young couples enjoy a stroll along Marine Parade.

The Avenue, Cliff Park, *c.* 1920. The avenue of holm oaks was formerly part of the grounds belonging to John Bagshaw's mansion. After the council obtained a lease on the grounds it was transformed into a park. The area was tastefully laid out with walks, parterres and fine rose beds. This was a popular venue in the summer months with bands, alfresco concerts, fireworks and fairylight displays. Note the magnificent pram in the foreground.

The Spa in 1912. It was hoped that this spa, opened in 1854, would rival those at Brighton and Tunbridge Wells but it was short lived and sold after Bagshaw's bankruptcy in 1859. During the First World War the spa was occupied by troops and the Corporation demolished it in 1920.

The beach and 'Donkey Hill', late 1890s. Sweet-scented tamarisk bushes covered the slopes and here the goat carts and donkeys plied their trade. Their daily routine was to ferry day-trippers up and down the hill. On the left is the undeveloped field where only Holland House stands. Quality houses were soon to be developed on this site.

The beach looking to the west, c. 1900. The many bathing machines and refreshment rooms were hired from the adjoining Phoenix Hotel. Shaftesbury Camp tents can be seen at the top of the picture. This whole area was transformed around 1925 when a new promenade was built and the boating lake, yacht pond, paddling pool and permanent amusements were introduced.

Builders working on sea defences and the new Promenade, c. 1923. The promenade extension, along with a new road and amenities, transformed the west end.

A postcard photograph of the same view in 1950 showing tennis courts, putting green and an extension of the promenade.

The beach and lighthouses, *c.* 1920. After the lighthouses at Harwich became unsafe as a leading mark into the harbour, due to shifting sands diverting the channel, these two Mitchell Screwpile lighthouses were erected and switched on in early November 1863. They were linked by a causeway, which was covered at high tide and remained in use until 1917. For a period the local Sea Scouts used the larger one as its headquarters and Tendring District Council eventually restored them. The pleasure boat jetty can be seen behind the inshore lighthouse.

The boating lake, *c.* 1928. Constructed at the same time as the extension to the promenade was being carried out around 1925, the lake proved to be a very popular attraction to summer visitors and locals alike. The tall chimney in the centre background is 'Pattrick's Shaft' some half a mile away.

The model yacht pond, 1938. Built around 1925, this pond soon became very popular and match races were organized on a regular basis. Teams would travel from all points of the south-east to take part. Such a race is in progress here, as two *Ganges* boys look on.

A crowded beach in the 1920s. The first bandstand, which was built by the Co-operative Society and presented to the community in 1902, is in evidence at the top left of the picture. A multitude of bands performed here, including those from HMS *Ganges*, the First Essex Volunteers and the Harwich Town Band.

The bandstand and new enclosure seen in 1930. The enclosure was erected and opened in July 1929 and provided more comfortable seating space together with a degree of protection from the bitter east winds, which often plague the promenade.

The New Band Pavilion, 1937. This structure retained the previously erected enclosure and the rock wall. It was supported by steel girders and the roof and sides were mainly of glass. The Pavilion was popular throughout the year, as only a little sunshine was required to lift the temperature inside. Calling in at the Pavilion's tea kiosk for a warming drink could make an autumn stroll along the promenade even more enjoyable.

A concert in the Cliff Pavilion 1937. The large uninterrupted floor space made this an ideal venue for dancing and concerts. Summer season entertainment was a regular feature here with dance bands and well known personalities performing, including Wilfred Pickles, David Nixon and Bob Monkhouse, to name but a few. The interior boasted glorious hanging baskets and beautiful climbing geraniums around the walls; the plants were well suited to the warm conditions. Unfortunately, during the late 1960s, the cliff slopes began to slide, some claim due to the removal of the tamarisk shrubs, the roots of which held the soil together. The council was forced to regrade the slopes, using this as an excuse for demolishing the Pavilion – a sad day.

The interior of the Cliff Pavilion, September 1936, on the occasion of the Electrical Exhibition where well known manufacturers such as Hotpoint, Hoover and English Electrics were displaying their most advanced equipment. As can be seen, the new building lent itself to this type of exhibition.

Mr Archer, beach inspector, with staff of the Cliff Pavilion, c. 1945. Mr Archer was also the town crier.

Four
Buildings

The interior of Cliff house, John Bagshaw's imposing mansion, built in 1845 and demolished in 1909.

Pattrick's cement works, early 1900s. John Pattrick, mayor and alderman of the town, produced both Roman and Portland cement here until 1906. There were five cement factories in the area in 1835, but by 1859 only Pattrick's remained. In 1871 he was prosecuted for emitting noxious gases and was forced to build a 320ft chimney shaft, known to locals as Pattrick's shaft. Labourers can be seen loading the trucks on the railway line running alongside the works. Pattrick sold out to Groom & Son in 1906 and the factory was eventually demolished in 1939.

The Towers in 1910, built by John Robson Pattrick, son of John, around 1885. The cement industry in Dovercourt became unprofitable around this time and Pattrick sold his house to Mr E.M. Jackson who set it up as a boarding school. In 1914 it became a military hospital for the duration of the war and from 1920 to 1971 it was taken over by the High School as a much needed annexe. HM Customs used the premises as a training centre from 1972 to 1982 and it is now the Towers Hotel.

The Kingsway Evangelical church in the 1930s undergoing repairs and repainting. The church was founded by Robert John Bagshaw and opened 23 August 1874 by Robert Baker. Built in the Italian style, the building is faced with Portland cement and was capable of seating 600-700 people. It had a tower of 80ft built in four stories and provision was made for a clock and bell. Three Venetian windows 12ft wide and 15ft high on each side, with one at each end, gave ample light, and under the whole building was a basement hall. The cost of the building was £2,400, exclusive of gas lighting, fencing and the value of the land. The church was sold in 1985 for conversion into an indoor market and has been recently taken over by Kingsway Hall Arts and Theatre Community Trust.

Cliff Road Congregational church, *c. 1930*. Services were originally held in the Victoria Hall, but after a time it was felt that a move to a separate building should be made. A large bazaar was held at the Retreat, which raised more than £200 and a site for a permanent church was sought. Donations and other funds raised resulted in the purchase of a site in Cliff Road. The foundation stone was laid in April 1908 and £4,000 was spent on the church, with a Sunday school in the under part. It has now been demolished and flats have recently been built on the site.

The Guildhall, Harwich in the 1920s. This impressive building with its Gothic door piece was erected in 1769 and had formerly been the Bear Inn. It replaced the previous Guildhall that had been in use since 1673. The council vacated it in 1951, moving to new premises in the former Great Eastern Hotel, after which the Guildhall became home to the YHA. Harwich Town council now has its offices here.

The isolation hospital, 1920s. Due to the poor sanitation of the 1860s, outbreaks of cholera and smallpox occurred and there were insufficient facilities available to accommodate the sick. After a number of deaths from smallpox in November 1879 it was decided an isolation hospital was necessary and this was opened in 1880. The hospital was also used for cases of scarlet fever and diphtheria until 1938, when the corporation took over the premises as a depot. The building is now used for small business starter units.

Borough of Harwich.

ISOLATION HOSPITAL.

Instructions for Relatives of Patients.

Name of Patient.

It is necessary to have as few Visitors as possible in a Fever Hospital, the Council therefore permit a Visit each Sunday and Wednesday Afternoons, from 3 p.m. to 4 p.m.

The production of this Card will secure admission to the Father, Mother, or other Adult Relative of the Patient (not more than Two Visitors).

Visitors may only see their Relatives through the windows, and are not allowed in the Wards except in cases where the Patient is dangerously ill, when the Matron may grant permission.

The Matron will notify the responsible Relative of a Patient if taken seriously ill. These Instructions are to be strictly observed.

A. J. H. WARD, Town Clerk.

Instruction card for relatives of patients at the isolation hospital, c. 1920. This gives an insight into the strict rules which visitors were expected to adhere to.

Warner's Holiday Camp, *c.* 1938. Captain Harry Warner formed 'Warner's in 1931 and went on to establish a public company in 1939. Dovercourt Holiday Lido was opened in 1937, attracting a good many holidaymakers from London and the home counties, who would very often return each year. From 1980 to 1987 the TV series Hi-De-Hi was filmed here, when the camp was transformed into 'Maplins' between summer seasons. Mr Warner planted the poplar trees surrounding the swimming pool itself. Unfortunately the camp closed its doors in 1990 and a housing estate now occupies the site.

Warner's holiday camp in 1990, after closure that summer. The overgrown gardens, desolate swimming pool and the fifty years old poplar trees are shown.

Hotel Alexandra, Marine Parade, mid-1950s. The hotel was opened in May 1903 and, with a frontage of 150 yards, it commanded fine views across the bay. It was luxuriously furnished and decorated, great care being taken to serve the best food. The function hall adjoining was used regularly for dances and concerts in the late 1950s, as shown by the billboards in the photograph. It is today a Methodist home for the elderly.

The Regal Cinema, *c.* 1940. It was opened by Ald. J. Cann JP on 1 June 1938 and advertised as 'a glorious rendezvous with all the enjoyment and comfort that could be anticipated, with air conditioning and using the latest Western electronic sound system'. Two films showing on the opening night were *100 Men and a Girl* starring Deanna Durbin, and *Two's Company* with Gordon Harker. Admission prices were 1s 8d and 1s 6d for the balcony and 1s 6d and 1s for the stalls. Falling attendances forced the Regal to change course and a bingo hall was established. After demolition in 1989 the site was left empty for several years until Alldays opened their present store here.

Seaview, the YMCA in Main Road situated at the corner of Alexandra Road, 1905. The YMCA used this house until the late 1920s, when it became a boarding house. The building remains unchanged today and is still called Seaview.

Regent Cinema, Main Road, opened in the 1920s. At the time it was claimed to be the largest in the district. It closed in the 1960s and is now used by Dolphin Sails, an established leading sailmaker.

The Cliff Hotel, overlooking the sea, *c.* 1895. Dovercourt's premier hotel has altered little exteriorly over the past 150 years. It began life in the 1850s as two houses (left) and shortly afterwards a coffee house was added to meet the demands created by John Bagshaw's plan to establish Dovercourt as a spa town. From then on it was known as the Cliff Hotel and some years later the Victoria Concert Hall was incorporated. The hotel soon ran into financial difficulties. However, after several changes of ownership it remains a first class hotel and is a popular venue for dances and exhibitions.

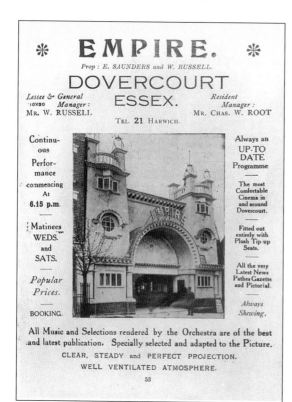

✻ EMPIRE. ✻

Prop : E. SAUNDERS and W. RUSSELL.

DOVERCOURT
ESSEX.

Lessee & General
10x90 Manager :
MR. W. RUSSELL.

Resident
Manager :
MR. CHAS. W. ROOT

TEL. **21** HARWICH.

Continuous
Performance
commencing
At
6.15 p.m.

Matinees
WEDS.
and
SATS.

Popular Prices.

BOOKING.

Always an
UP-TO
DATE
Programme

The most
Comfortable
Cinema in
and around
Dovercourt.

Fitted out
entirely with
Plush Tip-up
Seats.

All the very
Latest News
Pathes Gazette
and Pictorial.

Always Shewing.

All Music and Selections rendered by the Orchestra are of the best and latest publication. Specially selected and adapted to the Picture.

CLEAR, STEADY and PERFECT PROJECTION.
WELL VENTILATED ATMOSPHERE.

53

The Empire Cinema, Kingsway, seated 500 people and opened in 1913. This cinema was the first to close in 1938, when the Regal was opened and it remained empty until demolition in 1963. A small row of shops was then built on the site.

The Electric Palace Cinema in 1970. This is believed to be one of the oldest purpose-built cinemas in the country, complete with ornamental frontage. Built by Charles Thurston a well-known travelling showman, it opened 29 November 1912. After its closure in 1956, the cinema stood derelict until 1972 when a trust was formed to carry out restoration. This was done superbly and the Palace is once again showing films.

The Elco building, Marine Parade, was formerly Cliff Hall and is seen here in 1935. Built in the early 1900s with the holiday trade in mind, it had double-glazed windows, which were rare at the time. During the First World War the building was used as a hospital. Unfortunately it was little used during its lifetime, but WRNS were billeted here during the Second World War. It was for a time used as holiday flats but then became empty and remained for many years as an abandoned eyesore on the sea front.

The interior of the Elco in 1950 with Mr Elliott, the owner, in one of the large rooms. It was among the first buildings in the town to suffer from enemy action during the war. The building was finally demolished in August 1972 and replaced with accommodation for the elderly as Wimbourne House.

The High Lighthouse in the 1920s. A lighthouse has been on this site since 1664. General Rebow obtained a new lease in 1815 on both the High and Low lighthouses, provided that he rebuilt them at his own expense. Work started in 1817 and was completed in the spring of 1818, at a cost of more than £8,000. Both lighthouses had become obsolete by November 1863 and in 1909 the High Lighthouse was sold to Harwich Corporation and used for accommodation purposes until the late 1980s. The top balcony was removed during the 1930s and the lighthouse is at present 'home' to the National Wireless Museum.

The Low Lighthouse, seen here in 1916, was built in 1817 and used until 1863, by which time the tides had so shifted the sands that the approach to the harbour channel had changed. Trinity House vested the lighthouse to the Corporation in 1896 in return for the sum of 10s, but retained the right to use it should circumstances arise. The building was used as a Pilot Station during the late 1960s and '70s and is now the Harwich Maritime Museum.

This empty field, seen here in 1913, was to become the site for the new Sports Club and hard tennis courts. The foreman ground worker and his pets are pictured in the foreground while the footings for the new building are being dug out. Tents were erected to accommodate the workers.

Dovercourt Sports Club was opened 15 April 1912 and was founded through the enterprise of Mr B.J.S. Carlyon-Hughes who became its first Honorary Secretary. The aim of the club was to provide its members with a clubhouse and grounds for sporting purposes. Seven hard tennis courts were laid, making Dovercourt only the second in England to possess this many. By 1913 the club had a membership of 250, some drawn from the Dovercourt Lawn Tennis Club, although many were Royal Navy Officers stationed at Harwich. The clubhouse boasted oak-panelled décor, cushioned window seats and a tastefully equipped billiard room and card rooms. With well-prepared food, hot water baths and 'other refinements', the comfort of members was ensured. In 1925 Harwich Borough Council purchased the property for £5,115.

The Retreat, *c.* 1908. Built in a Swiss style in 1889 and situated in Beach Road, facing the beach and lighthouses, The Retreat was specially designed to accommodate large parties. Initially owned by J. Riggs, it was later taken over by W.F. and H. Gray and became known as Grays Retreat. Parties of London schoolchildren would spend their summer holidays here, taking advantage of the sports and leisure facilities on offer. The Retreat was requisitioned by the Army in the Second World War and was never to regain its former status. It was demolished in the early 1950s.

Five
Famous People and Local Characters

Endeavour in the 1934 Harwich Regatta. Tommy Sopwith, millionaire owner and regular visitor to Harwich talks tactics with local pilot Bert Good. Famous for the Sopwith Pup and the Sopwith Camel aircraft, Tommy Sopwith had this yacht built by Nicholson's of Southport to challenge for the Americas Cup. He used several modern aviation and engineering techniques on the rigging and hull, only to lose his challenge to Harold Vanderbilt sailing *Rainbow*. The series was won 4-2 to *Rainbow*. Sopwith tried his luck again in 1937 but again lost to Vanderbilt, 4-0.

Brittania, owned and raced by King George V, at the Harwich Regatta, after conversion to 'J'
Class standard in around 1934. Originally 'Gaff' rigged, it was a very successful racing yacht,
notching up 200 wins by 1930. After the death of George V in 1936 the yacht was stripped and
its equipment sold. It was then towed unceremoniously out to sea and scuttled off St
Catherine's point on the Isle of Wight. For this unique vessel, in perfect racing trim, to suffer
such a fate was sad indeed.

Sir Thomas Lipton, the tea millionaire, lifting a cup of tea made from his own blend, *c.* 1930. The young lady wishing him luck on his Americas Cup challenge is the film star Lois Moran. Sir Thomas was no stranger to Harwich and owned a shop in Market Street, The International Tea Company. Lipton had spent thirty years and millions of pounds trying to win the cup back for England.

New Cup challenger launched 14 April 1930 at Camper-Nicholsons yard at Gosport. Thomas Lipton (centre), Lady Shaftesbury and Charles Nicholson watched the *Shamrock* as it was launched. The *Shamrock* was the first 'J' class yacht to be built. The overall length was 120ft and the enormous mast was 160ft high and it weighed 3 tons. Alas *Shamrock* lost to Harold Vanderbilt's *Enterprise* 4-0. The *Shamrock* survives today and is presently undergoing restoration on the Isle of Wight.

John Bagshaw MP. Dovercourt owes much to this gentleman and his vision of a new spa town. The first part of his plan was to build Orwell Terrace and he was also responsible for laying out the Marine Parades as well as being partly instrumental in bringing the rail link to Harwich. Unfortunately John Bagshaw became bankrupt in 1859 and one wonders what fortunes Dovercourt would hold today had his dreams came to fruition. He died in 1861 and was succeeded by his son Robert, who also became an MP.

Commander Kerans and Herbert Wilcox at Harwich Quay in 1957, accompanied by Ralph and Rosemary Potts who were owners of the tender to the film crew. The filming of *The Yangtse Incident* took place on the River Orwell and HMS *Amethyst* was towed round to Harwich to re-enact the drama. The film tells the story of *Amethyst's* dramatic dash to freedom after being detained by the Chinese communists for 100 days. Commander Kerans was awarded the DSO for bravery in command of his ship, and was portrayed by Richard Todd in the film. Left to right: Rosemary Potts, Herbert Wilcox (director), Ralph Potts and Commander Kerans.

Arthur Chambers celebrates twenty-five years as publican of the Alma in 1978. Arthur spent fifty-five years behind the bar of the Alma Inn where his father was licensee from 1932 until 1953, when Arthur and his wife Peggy took over the pub. He retired in 1987 and now lives opposite the Alma in the house where Christopher Jones, captain of the *Mayflower*, once resided. Arthur and Peggy will be remembered for their generosity and charity work.

Len 'Goosey' Gostling DSM, 1912-1987. Len was one of life's colourful characters – his dry wit and wicked sense of humour made him unforgettable. He began his career on square rig sailing ships, serving in the Merchant Navy. Then starting as a 'fluonomist' (chimney sweep), he operated several small businesses in the town. As well as being a keen supporter of local charities, he helped rescue the victims of the 1953 flood. In 1940 Len was awarded the DSM when his lifeboat, full of survivors at Dunkirk, was left behind by its parent ship *Archangel* and there was no alternative but to row home to England. Before they got very far the lifeboat began to sink but luckily the men were picked up by the Dutch ship *Paschol* which then headed for Southampton.

Ralph Potts 1908-1996. Born in Reigate, Surrey, Ralph came to Harwich in 1946. He was invalided out of the Royal Navy after twenty years service. He and his wife Rosemary lived aboard an ex-RAF launch and began to offer river trips on their pleasure launch, *Yvonne*. This service continued until 1978 when Ralph 'came ashore' to Church Street, a stone's throw from the sea.

Six
Sport and Leisure

A photographer's nightmare! The local schools' music concert in the Cliff Pavilion in 1933. This event took place annually until the outbreak of war in 1939.

Harwich Radio and Cycles, 'Philco Radio Tableau', 1920. Gus Cheeseman, the proprietor, regularly entered floats for the carnivals, a tradition which his grandchildren carry on today. Including: Daphne Green, Christopher Green, Dorothy Cheeseman, John Cheeseman, Doris Potter, Mary Cheeseman and Frank Cheeseman.

George Bradford's Guy carnival float from 1933, depicting 'Pattrick's Shaft'. The huge chimney adjoining the cement works had become an eyesore and local opinion was that it should be demolished.

Life was returning to normal after the war in 1947 and here we have the *Daily Mail* sandcastle competition in progress on Dovercourt beach, near the Pavilion. Upper Dovercourt boys weigh up the opposition. The group on the left includes Terry Honeybell and the Mowle brothers.

A typical Len 'Goosey' Gostling Guy Carnival float, shortly after the war. Goosey dressed as a witch doctor is imprisoned in the cage, whilst his nephew, Peter, the waiter on the right, looks on.

The Harwich Salvation Army band, 1909. Front row, second from left is Capt. Ashwell, whose wife is next to the bass drummer.

K & K Fragmentos, 1922. This group of entertainers performed regularly at the Victoria Hall, Cliff Hotel.

Dovercourt Townswomen's Guild choir at a concert in the Cliff Pavilion in the 1950s. The conductor was Gladys Gooch.

Second World War veterans revive the 'Royal' darts team in 1946. Back row, left to right: Stokes, Mowle, Handscombe, Gladwin, and Whatling, -?-, -?-, -?-. Front row: -?-, Costorphin.

Dovercourt Corporation Band of the 1912 season, pictured at the Spa prior to a performance in Cliff Park. Front row, centre is W. Jones Blackett, conductor.

The Coronation of George V in 1911 allowed for celebrations all over the country. Here girls from the Harwich School are dressed up to celebrate in style.

Hill School teachers' football team in around 1949. Back row, left to right: 'Bruiser' Davies, 'Chalky' White, 'Gaffer' Johnson, Dobson, Tyler, 'Chippy' Chapman, Ted Smith (referee). Front row: Pike, 'Flash' Jones, Tommy England, Leonard, Charlie Penfold.

The Victor Ludorum at Harwich High School with an array of trophies, 1914.

Local building firm, Fisher and Woods' superb 1933 carnival float entry, depicting the *Mayflower* and the Pilgrim Fathers. It won first prize and the magnificent sum of £3.

Harwich Motor Cycle Club trial in Wrabness Woods, 1964. Left to right: -?-, Bob Fosker, Ken Field, Ray Harrison, Slony, John Culley, Eric Yallop, Maurice Everett, Tony Maslin, the Brand brothers, Mick Shaw.

Dovercourt beauties, 1933. A beauty contest at the first (and some would say the best) summer carnival organized by Mr Carlyon Hughes and Pattinsons, the large drapery store in Dovercourt. Left to right: Doris Thorne, Doreen Stead, -?-, 'King' Henry Curtis,' Queen' Hilda Dowling, -?-, Lily Harrison, Kathleen Falkoner, Chrissie Smith.

1934 saw another summer carnival and here are the 'King' Fred Pennick and the 'Queen' Muriel Wells with their court. Also pictured are the court jester, trumpeters and attendants.

Opening day for the new sports club, 15 April 1912. Some tennis players and committee members are pictured, prior to their first tournament. Back row, left, is the founder Mr Carlyon-Hughes.

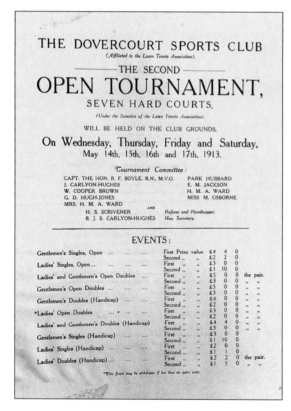

THE DOVERCOURT SPORTS CLUB
(Affiliated to the Lawn Tennis Association).

—————— THE SECOND ——————

OPEN TOURNAMENT,
SEVEN HARD COURTS,
(Under the Sanction of the Lawn Tennis Association).

WILL BE HELD ON THE CLUB GROUNDS,

On Wednesday, Thursday, Friday and Saturday,
May 14th, 15th, 16th and 17th, 1913.

Tournament Committee :

CAPT. THE HON. R. F. BOYLE, R.N., M.V.O.   PARK HUBBARD
J. CARLYON-HUGHES   E. M. JACKSON
W. COOPER BROWN   H. M. A. WARD
G. D. HUGH-JONES   MISS M. OSBORNE
MRS. H. M. A. WARD

H. S. SCRIVENER AND *Referee and Handicapper.*
B. J. S. CARLYON-HUGHES *Hon. Secretary.*

EVENTS :

Event		Prize	£	s	d	
Gentlemen's Singles, Open	... ...	First Prize value	£4	4	0	
		Second ,, ,,	£2	2	0	
Ladies' Singles, Open	... ...	First ,, ,,	£3	0	0	
		Second ,, ,,	£1	10	0	
Ladies' and Gentlemen's Open Doubles	....	First ,, ,,	£5	0	0	the pair.
		Second ,, ,,	£3	0	0	,, ,,
Gentlemen's Open Doubles	....	First ,, ,,	£5	0	0	,, ,,
		Second ,, ,,	£3	0	0	,, ,,
Gentlemen's Doubles (Handicap)	....	First ,, ,,	£4	0	0	,, ,,
		Second ,, ,,	£2	0	0	,, ,,
*Ladies' Open Doubles	.... *	First ,, ,,	£3	0	0	,, ,,
		Second ,, ,,	£2	0	0	,, ,,
Ladies' and Gentlemen's Doubles (Handicap)		First ,, ,,	£4	4	0	,, ,,
		Second ,, ,,	£3	0	0	,, ,,
Gentlemen's Singles (Handicap)	....	First ,, ,,	£3	0	0	
		Second ,, ,,	£1	10	0	
Ladies' Singles (Handicap)	....	First ,, ,,	£2	0	0	
		Second ,, ,,	£1	1	0	
Ladies' Doubles (Handicap)	... ...	First ,, ,,	£2	2	0	the pair.
		Second ,, ,,	£1	5	0	,, ,,

This Event may be withdrawn if less than six pairs enter.

A 1913 tournament card with a prize of 4 guineas for the gent's singles winner.

Football stars of the future? All Saints school team in 1949. Back row, left to right: Peter Gostling, Tony Casey, David Bird, John Mowle, Terry Gant, Steve Pike. Centre row: Herbert Farrow, David Bunting, Roger Stevens, Mervyn Hales, Reg Griggs. Front row: Peter Clover, Peter Kent, Cliff Farthing.

In 1953 Harwich and Parkeston football team reached the final of the FA Amateur Cup held at Wembley on 11 April. The picture shows one of the three special trains that were laid on for the Harwich supporters. Sixty coaches and numerous private cars made the journey to London. The local shops were closed and Harwich became a ghost town for the day. Unfortunately Harwich and Parkeston lost 6-0 to Pegasus, a combined university student team.

A group of schoolchildren from Mitcham in 1922, outside The Retreat on Dovercourt seafront.

Shaftesbury Camp in 1921. The huge open space at the west end of Dovercourt made a magnificent camping area. The 7th Earl of Shaftesbury set up this site especially for the underprivileged children of London.

Seven
Captain Fryatt

Capt. Charles Algernon Fryatt 1871-1916, master of SS *Brussels*. On 28 March 1915 SS *Brussels* was steaming from Harwich to the Hook of Holland when the German Sub U33 ordered her to stop. Capt. Fryatt increased to maximum speed, narrowly missing the submarine, and then began a game of cat and mouse with the U-boat, continually trying to stop the ship. Eventually the sub gave up. German submarines continued to harrass British shipping and on 22 June 1916 the *Brussels* was surrounded by German destroyers and the ship was sailed into Bruges under a German flag, where the crew were imprisoned and Capt. Fryatt interrogated. On 27 July 1916 he was brought before the court charged with attempting to ram the German submarine U33 and all he would say was, 'I have done nothing wrong'. The court found him guilty and two hours later he was taken to the prison yard, tied to a post and shot.

Upper
Dovercourt Churchyard.

Funeral of

Captain Charles Algernon Fryatt,

Master of the

Great Eastern Railway Company's

S.S. "Brussels,"

who was Murdered by the Germans,

July 27th, 1916, at Bruges, Belgium.

July 8th, 1919.

Service Sheet.

Captain Fryatt's body was brought home from Belgium 7 July 1919 and was taken to London on the following day. After a funeral service at St Paul's Cathedral the body left Liverpool Street Station on a special train to Harwich. A large procession gathered, consisting of GER staff, the mayor and corporation, representatives of the Navy and Army and various local groups. The streets were lined with thousands of onlookers wishing to pay their respects to this national hero. This photograph was taken outside All Saints school opposite the church. The choirboy carrying the cross was Christopher Pennick.

Capt. Fryatt's funeral cortège makes its way to the burial site at the lower end of All Saints churchyard, overlooking Parkeston Quay. Amongst the pallbearers are Capt. Barren, Capt. Stiff and Fryatt's friend and fellow skipper, Capt. Lawrence (the short man to the right of the coffin).

Capt. Fryatt's family inspect the floral tributes at the grave in All Saint's churchyard.

A handsome memorial stone provided by the Great Eastern Railway Company marks the grave.

Eight

Transport

An early 1930s Morris Commercial truck belonging to F. Kettle & Sons outside their bottling works in Gwynne Road. Kettle's earned several gold medals and diplomas for the quality of their mineral waters. They ceased trading in the 1980s and the premises have since been demolished and replaced with housing.

A Dovercourt Bay advertising van, around 1920 showing the Corporation's forward thinking method of advertising the town.

The 1922 White Hart pub outing to Clacton-on-Sea.

The International Stores delivery cart with George Nevard, the horseman, holding the reins, c. 1914.

'The Silver Queen' bus ready to depart for Clacton-on-Sea, with driver Freddie Butler, in 1929.

The Great Eastern Railway coach preparing for the local Harwich to Upper Dovercourt run in 1914.

Tricker's distinctive Model-T Ford, pork butcher's delivery van, parked at Harwich Quay, around 1920. Note the model of Tricker's 'pig' trademark on top.

Three local lasses pose on this motorcycle and side car outfit belonging to Wallis, a local photographer, c. 1920. The girl on the left is Gladys Gooch. Wallis produced numerous postcards and portraits, many of which have been used in the preparation of this book.

Dovercourt station, c. 1930. A group of businessmen ready to board the London train.

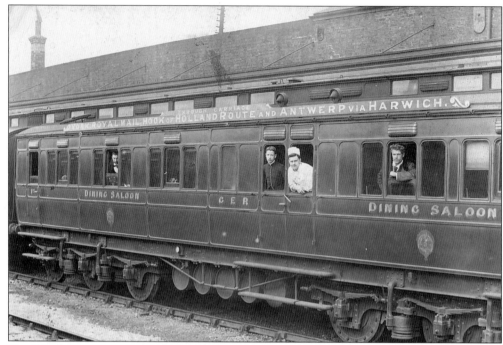

The 'Hook Continental' train at Parkeston Quay, waiting for passengers to disembark from the North Sea ferry, January 1898. In the centre of the dining saloon is Mr Manning (steward) next to Bob Walduck (chef).

Harwich fire brigade on parade during the Second World War with the Dennis fire engine and its crew. Back row, left to right: Joss Read, -?-, Harry Smith. Front row: Jack Good, Dick Thorpe, Lou Bowgen (chief) and Walter Fife.

Charras, owned by Leggett & Tricker, pictured at their depot in Kingsway, next to the church, c. 1925. The return fare to Clacton was 4s, with 'ride on air' comfort pneumatic tyres.

Leggett's light truck in Hill Road, mid-1920s. This truck was designed to carry both goods and passengers. St Augustine's church and church hall are visible in the background.

Harwich ambulance crew takes time off to be photographed with their vehicle during the Second World War. The ambulance was American made and is thought to be a Buick straight 8.

A picture of Leggett and Tricker's & Leggett's garage adjacent to Cliff Park, c. 1920. This garage began operation shortly after Cliff House was demolished and catered for the increase in numbers of motor vehicles. When the business was later moved to Kingsway, it became known as Leggett & Dyer.

Nine

Troubled Times

MV *Duke of York*, May 6 1953. The ship was on her way to Parkeston Quay with 470 passengers and crew in a thick fog when she was in a collision with the American ship *Haiti Victory*. The *Duke of York* had her bow section cut right off and the crew and passengers were taken aboard the *Haiti Victory, Norfolk Ferry* and *Dewsbury*. The tug *Empire Race* towed the *Duke of York* into Parkeston Quay and the ship was made watertight. Sadly eight lives were lost in the accident. She was repaired with a longer bow at Jarrow and resumed service in 1954.

MV *Kronprins Frederik* after arrival at noon 19 April 1953 at Parkeston Quay, Harwich. Her passengers were discharged shortly after a fire had broken out which burnt out the entire interior of the ship. Over 100 firemen fought the blaze but unfortunately so much water was used to put out the fire it caused the ship to roll over. There were no casualties.

Salvage vessels lifting and pumping out the MV *Kronprins Frederik*. The salvage operation took some time and she was eventually raised on 26 August 1953 and towed to Elsinore, Denmark for refitting on 13 September 1953. She re-entered service in May 1954.

The *Freija* in Harwich harbour in autumn 1942 salvaging sections of the ill-fated HMS *Gypsy*. Felixstowe hammerhead crane is in the background and there are barrage balloons overhead.

HMS *Gypsy* was a 'G' Class Destroyer. Steaming out of Harwich harbour on 21 November 1939 it hit a magnetic mine dropped by enemy aircraft. It broke her back and sank with the loss of over forty officers and men.

The flood of 1 February 1953. During the evening of 31 January the tide began rising to alarming heights. A gale was blowing and by 10 p.m., three hours before the predicted high tide, the water was lapping over the top of Harwich Quay. The sea defences were breached and Harwich was severely flooded, with some areas under 12ft of water. A Royal Navy diver searches the Main Road area at its junction with Fernlea Road.

An aerial view of Harwich on 2 February 1953 showing the extent of the east coast flood in which eight people lost their lives.

Rescuers move some elderly residents to safety as the floodwaters subside.

The mayor, councillors and officials inspect the emergency sandbag defences in the aftermath of the floods.

Emergency repairs under way in Main Road and West Street area, 1941. Very few roofs were left intact in the vicinity after a German bombing raid.

Numbers 18-20 Cliff Road in May 1941 were the scene of devastation after an evening bombing raid on 3 May of that year.

Beacon Hill bomb damage, 1941. Bombing raids over Harwich were at their height at this time and this picture shows the results of one such raid on 25 February. This bomb claimed five lives.

Children inspect damaged houses in Park Road following a Zeppelin raid, c. 1914.

An early morning scene as the fire brigade damp down the burnt out Phoenix Hotel, Lower Marine Parade in May 1914. A policeman on duty spotted the fire in the early hours and raised the alarm. As the building was constructed almost completely of wood the fire spread rapidly. The hotel was totally gutted but fortunately there were no casualties.

Staff inspect damage at the premises of C.H. Bernard & Sons clothing factory after a German bomb hit it on 17 May 1941.

Ten
Afterthoughts

Stirrup pumps, bells and clappers at the ready in 1941. A group of air-raid wardens from the Rosebank first-aid station, off Parkeston Road. Front row, third from the left is Jack Jones and fourth from the left, Walter Gooch.

Marine Shops Band pictured at Harwich Quay, c. 1930. This band performed regularly at carnival time when local charities benefited considerably from the money raised. Front row, third from left, we see one of the famous 'big heads'.

'We miss you Dad', Christmas 1914. This is an example of a wartime picture postcard, produced by local photographer Wallis, to be sent by children to their fathers serving abroad.

Little Eastern Ladies social club, *c.* 1930. The ladies gather outside the pub in readiness for their annual outing. Back row, left to right: Mrs Chapman, Rodgers, Scott, Wakefield, Davis. Front row: Mrs Roberts, White, Smith, Proom, Testa.

A great day in Harwich and Dovercourt in 1925 as the town celebrates the arrival of electric light to the towns.

The Chairman of the Borough Electric Lighting Committee, Alderman E. Saunders, and Mrs. Saunders request the pleasure of the Company of

Mr. Bennett

at the switching on of the Electric Current by Her Worship The Mayor at Dovercourt Station, on Wednesday, 21st January, 1925, at 4.30 p.m., and afterwards to tea on 1st floor of the premises of Messrs J. A. Saunders, Ltd. High Street.

R.S.V.P.

An Alma pub outing to Yarmouth in 1950. Bill Chambers, the publican, is on the right.

Post Office telegraph boy, William Barker, prepares for another speedy delivery, c. 1900.

The funeral of W. Gooch, landlord of the Victoria Hotel in the late 1920s. The picture shows the cortège leaving the hotel with a contingent of 'Buffs' in attendance wearing their regalia.

Wallis and Crees studio, Upper Dovercourt, c. 1920. Frederick Percy Wallis (1878-1924) began working at Gt. Oakley in 1905 and, after several moves he transferred his business to a studio in Lt. Oakley. His daughter Winifred helped with his work from 1918 after leaving school, and later became Mrs Crees. In 1920 Wallis was able to expand his business with a new Upper Dovercourt studio and photo-kiosk in Dovercourt. Wallis will be remembered for producing a wealth of photographic postcards of local interest. His early postcards were signed F. Wallis and after his daughter became a partner they were signed F. & W. Wallis. He died in 1924 leaving a widow and eight children.

Peck and sons, coal merchants, *c.* 1915. Charles Peck is pictured with his two young sons, Charlie and George, at the junction of Hall Lane and Fronks Road.

Samuel Pepys (1633-1703) MP for Harwich. The famous diarist began his career as Clerk to the Exchequer in 1659. As well as being MP for Harwich on two occasions, he was also Secretary for the Affairs of the British Navy and instigated the development of shipbuilding at the Navyard at the time of the Dutch wars.